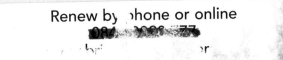

Fantastic Inventions and Inventors

By Zhu Kang

Illustrated by Hong Tao and Feng Congying

1. Paper-making
2. Moveable-type Printing
3. The Magic Compass
4. Gunpower

LONG RIVER PRESS
San Francisco

Copyright © 2005 Long River Press

Published in the United States of America by

LONG RIVER PRESS
360 Swift Avenue, Suite 48
South San Francisco, CA 94080
www.longriverpress.com

In association with Dolphin Books

Editor: Luo Tianyou

No part of this book may be reproduced without written permission of the Publisher.

ISBN 1-59265-039-2

Library of Congress Control Number: 2004113547

Printed in China

10 9 8 7 6 5 4 3 2 1

PAPER-MAKING

造纸

BEFORE THE INVENTION OF PAPER, VARIOUS METHODS AND MATERIALS WERE USED TO RECORD HISTORICAL EVENTS.

THE ANCIENT SUMERIANS CARVED CHARACTERS ON BOARDS MADE FROM COMPRESSED MUD.

THE ANCIENT EGYPTIANS WROTE ON PAPYRUS WHICH GREW ALONG THE BANKS OF THE NILE RIVER.

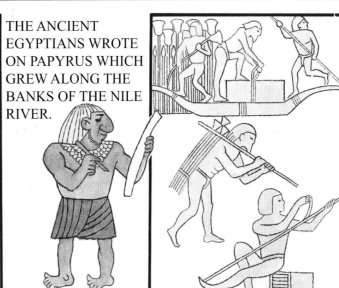

IN ANCIENT INDIA, PEOPLE WROTE ON PALM LEAVES.

EARLY EUROPEANS WROTE ON SHEEPSKINS.

ORACLE BONES

THESE INSCRIPTIONS WERE USED FOR PRACTISING DIVINATION. THEY ARE TORTOISE SHELLS OR ANIMAL SHOULDER BONES AND DATE FROM THE SHANG DYNASTY MORE THAN 3,000 YEARS AGO. THE SHELLS OR BONES WOULD BE PLACED IN THE FIRE AND THE BURN MARKS AND CRACKS WHICH RESULTED WOULD BE INTERPRETED AS SIGNS FROM HEAVEN.

2

THIS IS AN ANCIENT COOKING VESSEL WITH TWO LOOP HANDLES AND FOUR LEGS. THE CHARACTERS INSCRIBED ON IT ARE KNOWN AS "JI WEN," OR, "WRITINGS ON BRONZE."

JI WEN INSCRIPTION

CLANS AND TRIBES WERE CONSTANTLY AT WAR DURING THE PERIOD BEFORE THE SHANG DYNASTY, AS FAR BACK AS THE 17th CENTURY B.C.

3

AT THAT TIME THERE WAS NO PAPER. HISTORICAL RECORDS HAD TO BE CARVED OR INSCRIBED ON BONES, SHELLS, OR BRONZE VESSELS.

CUTTING BAMBOO

MAKING BAMBOO STRIPS

CHARACTER CARVING

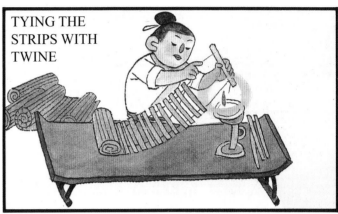

TYING THE STRIPS WITH TWINE

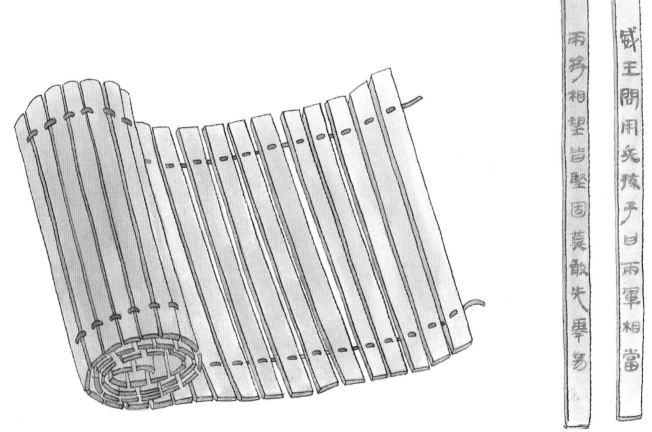

BT THE END OF THE SHANG DYNASTY (C.11TH CENTURY B.C.), PEOPLE BEGAN TO USE BAMBOO STRIPS AND WOODEN SLATS INSTEAD OF BONES AND SHELLS. IN THIS WAY WHOLE RECORDS OF HISTORICAL EVENTS COULD BE COMPILED.

5

THE BAMBOO STRIPS WERE HEAVY.
EVEN THE DAILY MEMORIALS READ BY THE
EMPEROR WEIGHED HUNDREDS OF POUNDS.

How do you like these p!um blossoms I painted?

Ah? Why do you paint on silk? It's far too expensive.

Bamboo is too heavy. Silk is too expensive.

We will find the answer.

6

THE BEST COCOONS ARE USED TO MAKE RAW SILK. THE INFERIOR QUALITY COCOONS ARE PLACED ON A STRAW MAT AND SOAKED WITH WATER. A WOODEN CLUB IS THEN USED TO FLATTEN THE SILK.

THE SILK FLOSS WAS DRIED UNDER THE SUN.

Auntie, are you making silk too?

I'm beating hemp which we will spin into yarn. We will make clothes with it.

Here. You can have these pieces to draw on.

MORE THAN 2,000 YEARS AGO, THE PEOPLE OF THE WESTERN HAN DYNASTY FOUND THAT AFTER COCOONS AND HEMP WERE BEATEN, A THIN LAYER OF FABRIC WAS FORMED ON THE MAT WHICH COULD BE USED AS WRITING MATERIAL.

DURING THE REIGN OF EMPEROR HE DI (89-105 A.D.) OF THE EASTERN HAN DYNASTY, CAI LUN INVENTED THE TECHNIQUE OF PAPERMAKING. AT THAT TIME, CAI LUN WAS AN OFFICIAL IN CHARGE OF THE IMPERIAL WORKSHOP.

I'm so tired of reading bamboo strips! How nice it would be if we could find something else to use.

The hemp and silk cocoons can be beaten flat. What about old bark, rags, and old fishing nets?

9

If we tear them into small pieces it will be easier.

THE PIECES OF BARK, RAGS, LINEN, AND OLD FISHING NETS WERE SOAKED IN WATER FOR SEVERAL WEEKS.

There are still some small pieces. We should pound them first then boil the mixture into pulp.

POUNDING WITH A STONE HAMMER.

BOILING OVER A BIG FIRE.

11

WHEN PAPER PULP IS POURED ON THE BAMBOO MOULD, IT SHOULD BE SPREAD THIN AND EVEN.

ALL WATER MUST BE PRESSED OUT.

DRYING PAPER SHEETS BY PLACING THEM ON THE WALL.

XU SHEN COMPILED THE FIRST DICTIONARY, *SHUO WEN JIE ZI* (ANALYTICAL DICTIONARY OF CHARACTERS) IN 100 A.D. IT INCLUDED THE WORD FOR "PAPER" AND EXPLAINED THAT PAPER WAS MADE OF SILK FLOSS.

PAPERMAKING DEVELOPED RAPIDLY FROM CAI LUN'S TECHNIQUE. MORE AND MORE MATERIALS WERE USED IN MAKING PAPER, AND THE SCALE OF THE PAPERMAKING INDUSTRY EXPANDED.

THE INVENTION OF THE TECHNIQUES OF PAPERMAKING IN CHINA GREATLY PROMOTED THE SPREAD OF CULTURE THROUGHOUT THE EMPIRE. PAPER WAS USED FOR WRITING AND CALLIGRAPHY, PAINTING, AND IN BOOK PRINTING.

MOVEABLE-TYPE PRINTING

活字印刷

BEFORE THE INVENTION OF THE PRINTING PRESS, BOOKS WERE COPIED BY HAND—A LABOR-INTENSIVE AND TIME-CONSUMING PROCESS.

There are so many characters! We can't possibly finish this before dark!

We have to or our master will be angry!

Oh! I feel dizzy and my back aches!

Hey, what are those people over there doing?

They are making rubbings from the stone tablet.

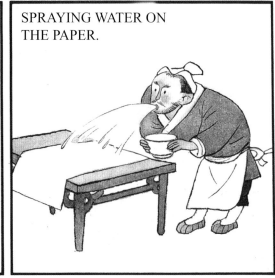

SPRAYING WATER ON THE PAPER.

THE PAPER IS PLACED SMOOTHLY ON THE STONE TABLET.

THE PAPER IS PRESSED ONTO THE INSCRIPTION. THE PAPER FITS INTO THE CARVINGS.

A BALL OF CLOTH IS DIPPED IN INK AND APPLIED TO THE PAPER. A RUBBING IS MADE.

This is a good method. Fast, and with no mistakes.

Could you make more for us?

THIS METHOD WAS SOON WIDELY USED AS A MEANS TO COPY CHARACTERS, PICTURES, AND INSCRIPTIONS.

THE USE OF SEALS BEGAN 3,000 YEARS AGO. SEALS WERE MADE OF WOOD, STONE, OR BONE. THE COLOR OF THE INK PASTE USED WITH THEM WAS RED.

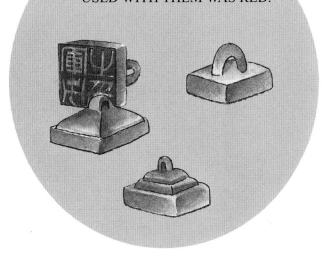

SU QIN, A POLITICIAN OF THE 4TH CENTURY BC, POSSESSED THE SEALS OF SIX STATES HANGING FROM HIS BELT.

THERE ARE TWO TYPES OF SEALS: YANGWEN, OR CHARACTERS CUT IN RELIEF; AND YINWEN, OR CHARACTERS CUT INTO THE SURFACE OF THE STONE (ALSO KNOWN AS INTAGLIO). YANGWEN CHARACTERS ARE RED ON A WHITE BACKGROUND, WHILE YINWEN CHARACTERS ARE WHITE ON A RED BACKGROUND.

YANGWEN   YINWEN

THE SIZE OF SEALS ALSO VARIED. FOR THE MOST PART THEY WERE SMALL. HOWEVER, THE LARGEST SEALS NEEDED TWO PEOPLE TO LIFT.

I'm looking for an auspicious blessing to display in my home.

I feel secure when I have this.

THE PRINTING PLATE WAS MADE OF WOOD ON WHICH CHARACTERS WERE CARVED.

We've worked so hard, but can carve only so many characters per day!

FEUDAL CULTURE FLOURISHED IN CHINA DURING THE TANG DYNASTY. THE DEMAND FOR BOOKS INCREASED, AND THE CARVING OF TABLETS AND SEALS COULD NO LONGER MEET THIS INCREASED DEMAND.

USING A PLANE TO SMOOTH A BOARD.

PLACING A WOODEN MATRIX ON THE BOARD.

CARVING CHARACTERS

A BRUSH, DIPPED LIGHTLY IN INK, GOES SMOOTHLY OVER THE BOARD.

PLACING A SHEET OF PAPER ON THE BOARD.

PRESSING THE PAPER USING A CLOTH PAD.

THUS, WOOD BLOCK PRINTING CAME INTO BEING AND SOON SPREAD THROUGHOUT THE EMPIRE. BY THE 9th CENTURY A.D. WOOD BLOCK PRINTING WAS WIDELY USED.

Two boards have been carved in less than one day!

It's much faster than stone carving, don't you think?

20

THE THOUSAND-
BUDDHA GROTTOES IN
DUNHUANG, LOCATED
FAR FROM THE TANG
CAPITAL.

Master, we have
finished carving
the Diamond
Sutra.

After several years, it
is complete at last!

The pieces of paper are
attached to one another
to form a scroll book!
Impressive!

21

THE DIAMOND SUTRA FEATURES THE INSCRIPTION: "THE TENTH DAY OF THE FOURTH LUNAR MONTH IN THE NINTH YEAR OF THE REIGN OF XIAN TONG."

HISTORIANS KNOW THIS DATE AS 868 A.D., WHICH PROVES THAT THIS BOOK IS THE EARLIEST PRINTED MATTER IN THE WORLD.

Your Excellency, the plates have arrived.

DURING THE MID-SONG DYNASTY, WOOD BLOCK PRINTING WAS WIDELY USED. BY THE END OF THE 11th CENTURY A.D., MORE THAN 100,000 PRINTING PLATES WERE PRESERVED IN THE IMPERIAL COLLEGE.

We must build a warehouse to store them all.

Already the warehouse is full! Where are we going to store all the plates?

22

DURING THE REIGN OF EMPEROR REN ZHONG OF THE SONG DYNASTY (1041-1048), BI SHENG INVENTED MOVEABLE TYPE PRINTING. IT WAS AN IMMENSE LEAP FORWARD IN THE DEVELOPMENT OF PRINTING TECHNIQUES AND WOULD HAVE AN IMPACT WORLDWIDE.

BI SHENG WAS FROM A POOR FAMILY AND FISHED TOGETHER WITH HIS FATHER WHEN HE WAS A CHILD.

You must study hard to learn methods of printing.

AFTER SEVERAL YEARS, BI SHENG HAD MASTERED ENGRAVING.

Ai! A single mistake ruins the entire plate!

There must be a solution.

REMOVING THE MISTAKE...

...MAKING A CORRECTION

Bi Sheng! This is a good method!

Master, if we engrave EACH character separately, we can assemble them for printing, then take them apart for later use. It will save lots of time and effort.

How do we hold all the pieces together?

Rosin and wax.

Bi Sheng! It's fantastic.

It's "moveable-type" printing.

CHARACTERS ENGRAVED USING WOOD WORE OUT OVER TIME, AND THE CONSTANT USE OF ROSIN AND WAX MEANT THE CHARACTERS HAD TO BE CLEANED THOROUGHLY AFTER REPEATED USE.

What can we use to replace wood?

My dice are better than yours!

Mine are better!

CERAMIC CHARACTERS WERE CARVED FROM CLAY AND FIRED FOR HARDNESS. IT WAS EASY TO ENGRAVE ON CLAY, AND THE CLAY TYPE DIDN'T LOSE ITS SHAPE EVEN AFTER REPEATED USE. THE CLAY TYPE WAS EASY TO ASSEMBLE AND DISASSEMBLE. IN THIS WAY MOVEABLE-TYPE PRINTING HELPED TO FURTHER SHORTEN THE PRINTING PROCESS.

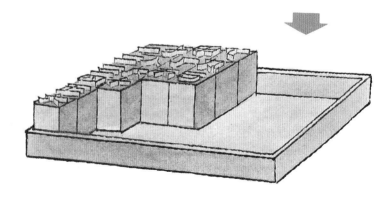

BY THE YUAN DYNASTY (1271-1368), WANG ZHEN, A NOTED AGRONOMIST, DEVELOPED A PROCESS BY WHICH CHARACTERS WERE PRESSED AND HELD TIGHTLY AGAINST THE PAPER BY BAMBOO STRIPS. THE RESULT WAS AN EXTREMELY CLEAR AND HIGHLY DETAILED METHOD OF PRINTING.

WANG ZHEN INVENTED THE REVOLVING TYPE FRAME. IT WAS MADE OF TWO WOODEN FRAMES WITH A DIAMETER OF APPROXIMATELY SIX FEET. BECAUSE THE FRAMES ROTATE, ONE FRAME WAS USED TO ACTUALLY SET THE TYPE IN THE WORK TO BE PRINTED, WHILE THE OTHER WHEEL SERVED AS A RECEPTACLE TO STORE VARIOUS BLOCKS OF TYPE BEFORE AND AFTER USE.

THE HISTORY AND
EVOLUTION OF PRINTING
FROM RUBBINGS,
SEALS, WOOD BLOCK
AND MOVEABLE TYPE
WAS A LONG PROCESS.
THE DEVELOPMENT OF
PRINTING IS DIRECTLY
LINKED TO THE SPREAD OF
ART, HISTORY, PHILOSOPHY,
AND CULTURE IN CHINA.

THE MAGIC COMPASS

指南针

DURING THE QIN DYNASTY (221-206 B.C.), EMPEROR QIN SHI HUANG UNIFIED CHINA. HIS PALACE WAS LOCATED IN XIANYANG, SHAANXI PROVINCE. BECAUSE OF HIS IRON-FISTED RULE, HE LIVED IN FEAR OF ASSASSINATION.

So many people died building the palace for this despotic emperor!

Kill him!

Right. Kill him!

THE EMPEROR'S GATE WAS AN IMMENSE
MAGNET AND NO METAL WEAPON COULD
PASS THROUGH. THE SCIENCE OF MAGNETS
LIES AT THE HEART OF THE MAKING OF THE
COMPASS.

THE SHAPE OF THESE MAGNETS IS DIFFERENT.
AT THE ENDS OF EACH MAGNET ARE TWO
DIFFERENT MAGNETIC POINTS, ALSO KNOWN
AS POLES.

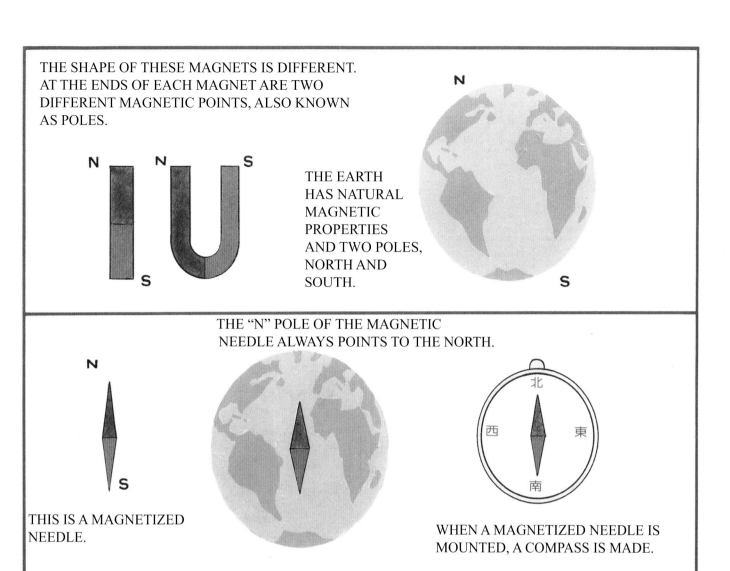

THE EARTH
HAS NATURAL
MAGNETIC
PROPERTIES
AND TWO POLES,
NORTH AND
SOUTH.

THE "N" POLE OF THE MAGNETIC
NEEDLE ALWAYS POINTS TO THE NORTH.

THIS IS A MAGNETIZED
NEEDLE.

WHEN A MAGNETIZED NEEDLE IS
MOUNTED, A COMPASS IS MADE.

THE ANCIENT COMPASS IS DIFFERENT FROM THE MODERN
COMPASS. THIS IS AN ANCIENT CHINESE COMPASS CALLED
SI NAN, USED DURING THE WARRING STATES PERIOD (475-221 B.C.).
IT RESEMBLES A SPOON SITTING ATOP A SQUARE WOODEN BOARD.

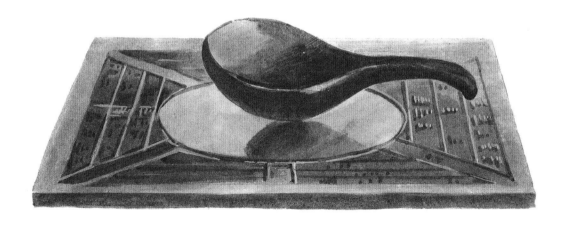

IN ANCIENT TIMES WHEN PEOPLE WENT TO DIG FOR JADE IN THE MOUNTAINS, THEY ALWAYS BROUGHT A *SI NAN* WITH THEM SO THEY DID NOT LOSE THEIR WAY.

32

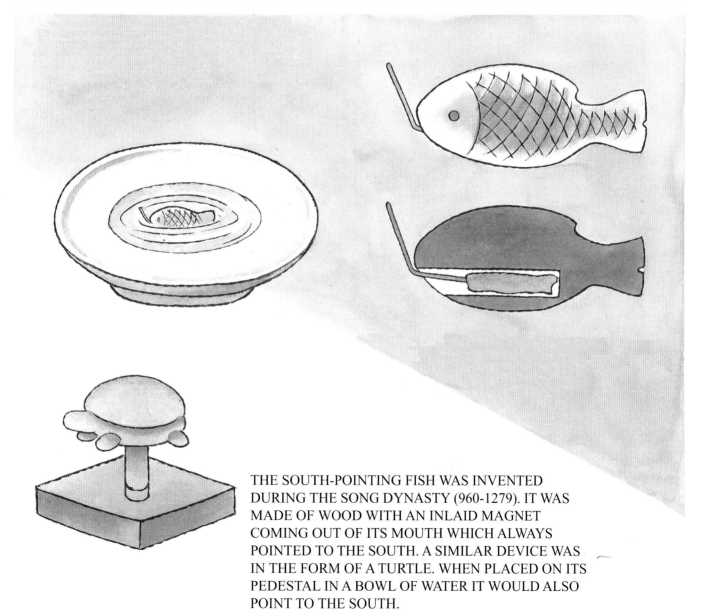

THE SOUTH-POINTING FISH WAS INVENTED
DURING THE SONG DYNASTY (960-1279). IT WAS
MADE OF WOOD WITH AN INLAID MAGNET
COMING OUT OF ITS MOUTH WHICH ALWAYS
POINTED TO THE SOUTH. A SIMILAR DEVICE WAS
IN THE FORM OF A TURTLE. WHEN PLACED ON ITS
PEDESTAL IN A BOWL OF WATER IT WOULD ALSO
POINT TO THE SOUTH.

IN THE 10TH CENTURY, A SOUTH-POINTING FISH MADE OF IRON WAS USED IN WARFARE. THERE WAS NO MAGNET IN THE BODY OF THE FISH, YET THE FISH ALWAYS POINTED TO THE SOUTH.

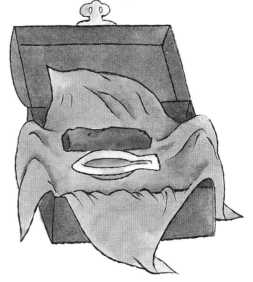

THE BOX CONTAINING THE IRON FISH ALSO HELD NATURAL MAGNETIC ROCK. WHEN THE ROCK AND THE IRON FISH WERE PLACED TOGETHER IN THE BOX FOR EXTENDED PERIODS, THE MAGNETIC PROPERTIES OF THE ROCK WERE ABSORBED BY THE FISH.

SHEN KUO WAS A NOTED SCIENTIST OF THE SONG DYNASTY AND THE AUTHOR OF THE *MENG XI BI TAN* (DREAM STREAM ESSAYS). SHEN KUO WROTE OF FOUR METHODS ENABLING A NEEDLE TO POINT TO THE SOUTH:

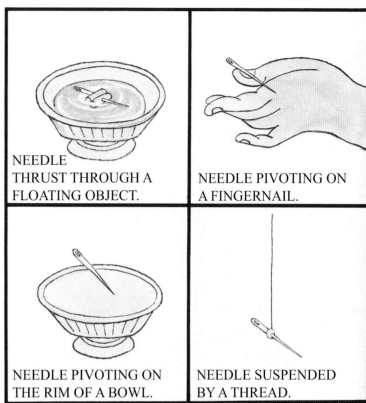

NEEDLE THRUST THROUGH A FLOATING OBJECT.

NEEDLE PIVOTING ON A FINGERNAIL.

NEEDLE PIVOTING ON THE RIM OF A BOWL.

NEEDLE SUSPENDED BY A THREAD.

SHEN KUO ALSO DISCOVERED MAGNETIC DEVIATION, WHICH IS THE DIFFERENCE BETWEEN TRUE NORTH AND MAGNETIC NORTH

35

THE INVENTION OF THE MAGNETIC COMPASS GREATLY HELPED THE DEVELOPMENT OF NAVIGATION. FROM THE 10TH CENTURY TO THE 17TH CENTURY, CHINESE FLEETS OFTEN SAILED ACROSS THE SOUTH CHINA SEA AND INDIAN OCEANS TO AFRICA AND THE MIDDLE EAST.

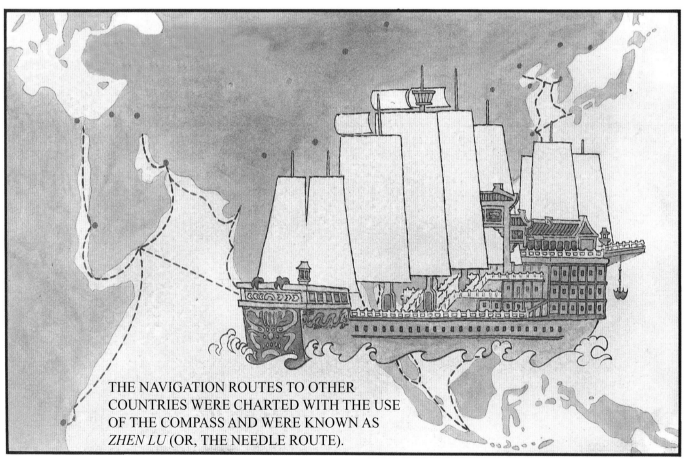

THE NAVIGATION ROUTES TO OTHER COUNTRIES WERE CHARTED WITH THE USE OF THE COMPASS AND WERE KNOWN AS ZHEN LU (OR, THE NEEDLE ROUTE).

GUNPOWDER

火药

IN ANCIENT TIMES, TAOIST ALCHEMISTS DREAMT OF MAKING GOLD FROM BASE METALS OR CREATING PILLS OF IMMORTALITY.

THEY PERFORMED COUNTLESS DIFFICULT AND DANGERIOUS EXPERIMENTS USING VARIOUS PLANTS, STONES, AND ELEMENTS FOUND IN NATURE.

THREE DAYS LATER.

SALTPETRE AND SULPHUR WERE AMONG THE BEST MEDICINES, BUT CHARCOAL MIXED WITH SALTPETRE AND SULPHUR WERE THE BASIC INGREDIENTS OF GUNPOWDER.

AFTER MANY DANGERIOUS EXPERIMENTS, THE CORRECT PROPORTIONS OF SALTPETRE, SULPHUR, AND CHARCOAL WERE DETERMINED. STARTING FROM THE 9th CENTURY, GUNPOWDER WAS USED IN WARFARE.

AT THE END OF THE TANG DYNASTY, THERE WAS GREAT SOCIAL DISORDER AND MUCH MILITARY CONFLICT.

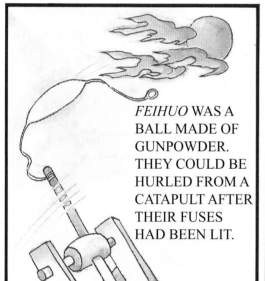

FEIHUO WAS A BALL MADE OF GUNPOWDER. THEY COULD BE HURLED FROM A CATAPULT AFTER THEIR FUSES HAD BEEN LIT.

41

FROM THE 11th TO THE 13th CENTURIES, THE GOVERNMENT OF THE SONG DYNASTY BUILT GUNPOWDER WORKSHOPS IN KAIFENG.

IN 1161, LED BY THE EMPEROR OF THE STATE OF KIN, 600,000 SOLDIERS CROSSED THE YANGTZE RIVER. THE TROOPS OF THE SOUTHERN SONG DYNASTY MET THEM HEAD ON.

Put the *pilipao* on the boats. Your shots must be accurate.

Yes sir!

Shall we open fire?

A little closer…

42

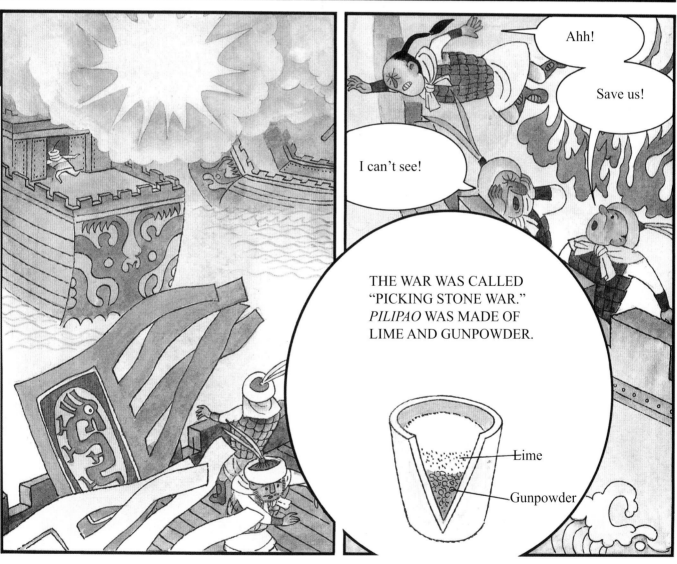

43

WHOOSH!

Master, how does your *huoqiang* work?

It's pretty accurate. Let me show you.

IN 1132, CHEN GUI INVENTED THE *HUOQIAO*, OR FIRE LANCE. IT WAS MADE OUT OF A THICK BAMBOO TUBE. LATER IT DEVELOPED INTO THE *HUOCHONG* (FIRE GUN), A PRECURSOR TO THE MODERN-DAY CANNON.

Incredible!

Wonderful!

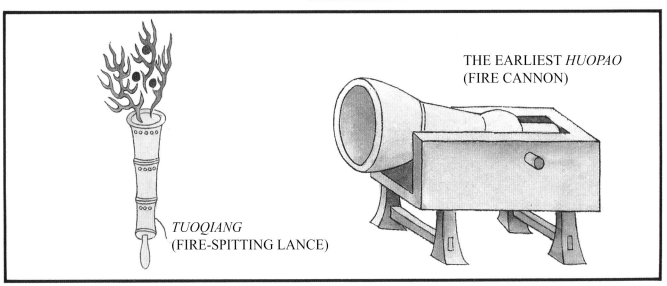

TUOQIANG
(FIRE-SPITTING LANCE)

THE EARLIEST *HUOPAO*
(FIRE CANNON)

FOLLOWING THE DEVELOPMENT OF GUNPOWDER, FIREARMS GRADUALLY IMPROVED. ROCKETS MADE IN THE 10th CENTURY HAD TO BE SHOT WITH A BOW AND ARROW. LATER, ROCKETS WERE FIRED AND PROPELLED BY A GUNPOWDER CHARGE.

IN THE 14th CENTURY, A TYPE OF ROCKET APPEARED WHICH RESEMBLED A KITE IN THAT IT COULD BE GUIDED DIRECTLY OVER THE ENEMY POSITION.

FEI KONG ZHEN TIAN LEI (FLYING CANNON).

HUO LONG CHU SHUI (FIERY DRAGON EMERGING FROM WATER).

SHEN HUO FEI YA (MAGIC FLYING FIRE CROW).

45

AT THE END OF THE 14th CENTURY, AN OFFICIAL OF THE MING DYNASTY HAD A FANTASTIC IDEA:

Since gunpowder can send rockets to the sky…

If I tie this rocket to my chair, I can fly as well.

Light the fuse! I have these two kites, so I can glide back to earth.

LIKE ICARUS, THE OFFICIAL FAILED IN HIS ATTEMPT TO FLY. NEVERTHELESS, HIS VISION WAS PROPHETIC. THOUGH MANKIND HAS YEARNED TO FLY WITH THE BIRDS, TODAY WE RELY ON AIRPLANES AND SPACECRAFT.

46